The White Stone

Selections from George MacDonald

To him who overcomes will I … give a white stone,

and in the stone a new name written,

which no one knows, except the one who receives it.

—Revelation 2:17

DEEP
THOUGHTS
IN A
NUTSHELL

The White Stone

Selections from George MacDonald

Compiled by Ellyn Sanna

ANAMCHARA BOOKS

The White Stone: Selections from George MacDonald

compiled by Ellyn Sanna

Anamchara Books
220 Front Street
Vestal, NY 13850

First Printing

9 8 7 6 5 4 3 2 1

ISBN: 978-1-937211-19-6
ebook ISBN: 978-1-937211-20-2

Library of Congress Control Number 2011909827

Cover design by Ellyn Sanna.
Interior design by Camden Flath.
Printed in the United States of America.

Although all selections are taken from various writings of George MacDonald, in some cases MacDonald's original text has been edited slightly to allow for gender-inclusive language or modern phrasing. All such edits were made in the spirit of MacDonald's original meaning and philosophy.

Contents

Introduction

George MacDonald was a mystic, a prolific author, and a theological rebel. He was also a loving father and husband, as well as a clergyman who was unable to keep a job. But it was his belief in Jesus Christ as a living person that shaped each of the other aspects of his life.

He was born in Scotland in 1824, the son of a farmer. His family attended the Congregational Church, a Calvinist denomination that believed in the doctrine of predestination (that God has chosen the "elect" for salvation, while others will be condemned to hell). MacDonald is said to have burst into tears as a young boy when someone explained this doctrine to him, despite the fact that he was assured he was among the elect.

As a young man, MacDonald earned a degree at the University of Aberdeen and then went Highbury College in London to prepare for ministry in the Congregational Church. In 1850, he was appointed pastor at the church in Arundel, West Sussex, but because his sermons insisted that God's love is relentless, pursuing human beings for all eternity, his salary was cut in half. He was repeatedly accused of heresy, and after three years, he resigned.

In 1851, MacDonald married Louisa Powell. They had six sons and five daughters together, and supporting his large family became MacDonald's greatest challenge: he preached, taught, tutored, and wrote novels that were the bestselling romances of his day—and still, he often needed to rely on the charity of his friends.

Never a worldly success, MacDonald still influenced many of the world's greatest writers and thinkers. Lewis Carroll, John Ruskin, Tennyson, Dickens, Wilkie Collins, Trollope, Lewes, Thackeray, Longfellow, Walt Whitman, and Lady Byron were all his friends. After MacDonald's death, W. H. Auden, C. S. Lewis, G. K. Chesterton, and J.R.R. Tolkien all counted his writing as an important influence on their thinking.

During MacDonald's lifetime, his romantic novels were his bread-and-butter, but it was his fantasies and sermons that have best survived the test of time. His best-known works—*The Princess and the Goblin*, *The Princess and Curdie*, *At the Back of the North Wind*, *Phantastes*, and *Lilith*—laid the foundation for a genre of writing upon which authors like C. S. Lewis and Madeleine L'Engle would later build. "I write, not for children," MacDonald said, "but for the childlike, whether they be five, or fifty, or seventy-five."

Throughout his life, in all his creative and professional endeavors, MacDonald steadfastly rejected the doctrine of substitutionary atonement—the concept that Christ's death was necessary in order to appease the wrath of a vengeful God. The idea that God could be anything but love was the true heresy, MacDonald insisted; the Divine as revealed by Christ, a God of total love and giving, was the only God in which MacDonald believed—and he believed in this God of love utterly, with his entire being.

MacDonald's belief was not a watery, undemanding sort of theology. Love is the ultimate challenge; it demands that we become our true selves, a process that is often painful, that requires everything from us. The surgeon's knife may be excruciating—but it only cuts in order to heal.

This is a theology that has seldom been taught by the established Church, and yet it is a quiet, biblical vein of thought that has never been totally repressed. The early Church Fathers— Clement of Alexandria, Origen, Gregory of Nyssa—believed in universal salvation. That changed with the establishment of Augustinian theology as the church norm, and alternative perspectives (for instance, that of Pelagius, the Celtic theologian) were labeled heresy. Confidence in the supremacy of God's love and the ultimate wholeness of the human soul continued to run through the revelations of the great medieval mystics, however, including Julian of Norwich, John of the Cross, and the author of the *Cloud of Unknowing*. And in the twenty-first century, Pastor Rob Bell caused a stir in the evangelical world by insisting that "love wins."

The doctrine of universal salvation remains a controversial one. Those who believe in it tend to do so quietly, for fear of offending the rest of the Christian world. George MacDonald had no such scruples. Instead, he believed wholeheartedly that a faith in anything other than a God of total love was the heresy. He wrote:

> The notion that a creature born imperfect, nay, born with impulses to evil not of his own generating, and which he could not help having, a creature to whom the true face of God was never presented, and by whom it never could have been seen, should be thus condemned, is as loathsome a lie against God as could find place in heart too undeveloped to understand what justice is, and too low to look up into the face of Jesus. . . . There is but one thing lower than deliberately to believe such a lie, and that is to worship the God of whom it is believed. . . . The work of Jesus Christ on earth was the creative atonement, because it works atonement in every heart.

He brings and is bringing God and man, and man and man, into perfect unity: "I in them and thou in me, that they may be made perfect in one."

"That is a dangerous doctrine!"

More dangerous than you think to many things—to every evil, to every lie, and among the rest to every false trust in what Christ did, instead of in Christ himself.

This book, *The White Stone*, contains short selections from MacDonald's writing, including his sermons, romances, and fantasies, arranged thematically. Each page-long thought is intended to be read slowly, one at a time, and pondered. This is the sort of book that's meant to be picked up for five minutes and put down again, while a kernel of insight takes root in your mind throughout the day.

And in the words of C. S. Lewis, Anamchara Books would also say of George MacDonald:

I know hardly any other writer who seems to be closer, or more continually close, to the Spirit of Christ Himself. Hence his Christ-like union of tenderness and severity. Nowhere else outside the New Testament have I found terror and comfort so intertwined. . . . In making this collection I was discharging a debt of justice.

I

The White Stone:
Our True Identity

To him who overcomes will I ... give a white stone,

and in the stone a new name written,

which no one knows, except the one who receives it.

—Revelation 2:17

To the one who offers unto this God of the living the own self of sacrifice, to the one who overcomes, the one who has brought the individual life back to its source, *this* one of the Father's making, God gives the white stone. To the one who climbs on the stair of all the God-born efforts and God-given victories up to the height of individual being—that of looking face to face upon the ideal self in the bosom of the Father—the *self* God created, realized in that person through the Father's love in the Elder Brother's devotion—to that person God gives the new name written on the white stone.

"God has cared to make me for himself,"

says the victor with the white stone,

"and has called me that which I like best."

Such a name cannot be given
until the person IS the name.

It is only when the person has become the name that God gives the stone with the name upon it, for only then can the person understand what that name signifies. It is the blossom, the perfection, the completion, that determines the name; and God foresees that from the first, because God made it so; but the tree of the soul, before its blossom comes, cannot understand what blossom it is to bear, and could not know what the word meant, which, in representing its own unarrived completeness, named itself.

No one but God sees what the person is.

God's name for a person must then be the expression in a mystical word—a word of that language which all who have overcome understand—of God's own idea of the person, that being whom God had in mind when God began to make the child, and whom God kept in mind through the long process of creation that went to realize the idea. To tell the name is to seal the success—to say, "In thee also I am well pleased."

The true name is one which expresses the character, the nature, the being, the *meaning* of the person who bears it. It is the person's own symbol—the soul's picture, in a word—the sign which belongs to that person and to no one else. Who can give a person this name? God alone.

And for each God has a different response. With every person God has a secret—the secret of the new name. In every person there is a loneliness, an inner chamber of peculiar life into which God only can enter. I say not it is *the innermost chamber*—but a chamber into which no brother, nay, no sister can come.

From this it follows that there is a chamber also—(O God, humble and accept my speech)—a chamber in God into which none can enter but the one, the individual, the peculiar person—out of which chamber that person has to bring revelation and strength for others.

> This is that for which each person was made—
> to reveal the secret things of the Father.

By creation, then,

each person is isolated with God.

Each, in respect of the peculiar making, can say, "*my* God"; each can come to God alone, and speak with God face to face, as a person speaks with a friend. There is no *massing* of people with God. When God speaks of gathered humanity, it is as a spiritual *body*, not a *mass*. For in a body every smallest portion is individual, and therefore capable of forming a part of the body.

Each of us is a distinct flower or tree in the spiritual garden of God—precious, each for our own sake, in the eyes of the One who is even now making us—each of us watered and shone upon and filled with life, for the sake of our flower, our completed being, which will blossom out of each of us at last to the glory and pleasure of the great Gardener. Each is growing toward the revelation of that secret to ourselves, and so to the full reception, according to our measure, of the divine. Every moment that we are true to our true selves, some new shine of the white stone breaks on our inward eyes, some fresh channel is opened upward for the coming glory of the flower, the conscious offering of our whole being in beauty to the Maker.

Each of us has within us a secret of the Divinity.

Life and action, thought and intent,

are sacred.

And what an end lies before us! To have a consciousness of our own ideal being flashed into us from the thought of God! Surely for this may well give way all our paltry self-consciousnesses, our self-admirations and self-worships! Surely to know what God thinks about us will pale out of our souls all our thoughts about ourselves! and we may well hold them loosely now, and be ready to let them go.

II

The Consuming Fire:
Divine Creativity

God's love burns away all that is not Pure,

all that is not as it was meant to be,

all that is not truly Real.

The consuming fire is just the original,

the active form of Purity—that which makes pure,

that which is indeed Love,

the creative energy of God.

Without purity there can be as no creation,

and so no persistence.

That which is not pure is corruptible.

The person whose deeds are evil, fears the burning.

But the burning will not come the less if we fear it or deny it.

Escape is hopeless. For Love is inexorable.

Our God is a consuming fire.

But at length, O God,

will you not cast Death and Hell into the lake of Fire—

even into your own consuming self?

Death shall then die everlastingly.

God is life, and the will-source of life. In the outflowing of that life, I know God; and when I am told that God is love, I see that if the Divinity were not love, God would not, could not create. I know nothing deeper in God than love, nor believe there is in God anything deeper than love—nay, that there can be anything deeper than love.

> The being of God is love,
>
> and therefore creation.

III

The Ongoing Creation

The whole universe is "tented" with love.

I repent me of the ignorance

wherein I ever said that God made humans out of nothing:

there is no nothing out of which to make anything;

God is all in all,

and Divinity made us

out of Divinity.

Each unique thing we see in Creation is divine truth.

There is no water in oxygen, no water in hydrogen: it comes bubbling fresh from the imagination of the living God, rushing from under the great white throne of the glacier. The very thought of it makes one gasp with an elemental joy no metaphysician can analyze. The water itself, that dances, and sings, and slakes the wonderful thirst—symbol and picture of that draught for which the woman of Samaria made her prayer to Jesus—this lovely thing itself, whose very wetness is a delight to every inch of the human body in its embrace—this live thing which, if I might, I would have running through my room, yea, babbling along my table—this water is its own self its own truth, and is therein a truth of God.

The God who is ever uttering the Divine Nature in the changeful profusions of nature; who takes millions of years to form a soul that shall understand Divinity and be blessed; who never needs to be, and never is, in haste; who welcomes the simplest thought of truth or beauty as the return for seed God sowed upon the old fallows of eternity, who rejoices in the response of a faltering moment to the age-long cry of divine wisdom in the streets; the God of music, of painting, of building, the Lord of Hosts, the God of mountains and oceans; whose laws go forth from one unseen point of wisdom, and thither return without an atom of loss; the God of history working in time . . . this God is the God of little children.

A healthy child's heart

holds within it the secret of Creation.

Creation is the ongoing revelation

of the heart of God.

If you think of ten thousand things that are good and worth having, what is it that makes them good or worth having but the God in them? That the loveliness of the world has its origin in the making will of God, would not content me; I say, the very loveliness of it is the loveliness of God, for its loveliness is God's own lovely thought, and must be a revelation of that which dwells and moves in God.

The whole system of the universe

works upon this law—

the driving of things upward

toward the center,

an ongoing process

that has no end.

IV

Human Love:
Our Relationship to the Other

The more we love our brother and our sister,

the more we shall know God.

For we are made for love,

not for self.

Our neighbor is our refuge;

SELF is our demon-foe.

Each person is the image of God to all people,

and in proportion as we love the individual,

we shall know the sacred fact.

Each person for whom we can do anything is our neighbor,

therefore, each of the human race who comes

within the touch of one tentacle of our nature

is our neighbor.

"Yes; but I cannot get into his consciousness, nor he into mine. I feel myself, I do not feel him. My life flows through my veins, not through his. The world shines into my consciousness, and I am not conscious of his consciousness. I wish I could love him, but I do not see why. I am an individual; he is an individual. My self must be closer to me than he can be. Two bodies keep me apart from his self. I am isolated with myself."

Now, here lies the mistake at last. While the thinker supposes a duality in herself which does not exist, she falsely judges the individuality a separation. On the contrary, it is the sole possibility and very bond of love.

OTHERNESS

is the essential ground of affection.

The love that enlarges not its borders,

that is not ever spreading and including, and deepening,

will contract, shrivel, decay, die.

I have had the sons and daughters of my mother that I may learn the meaning of the universal family. For there is a bond between me and the most wretched liar that ever died for the murder he would not even confess, closer infinitely than that which springs only from having one father and mother.

True, and thank God! the greater excludes not the less; it makes all the weaker bonds stronger and truer, nor forbids that where all are brothers, some should be those of our bosom. Still my brother and sister according to the flesh are my first neighbors, that we may be very nigh to each other, whether we will or no, while our hearts are tender, and so may learn *family.*

Then my second neighbor appears, and who is he? Whom I come in contact with whatsoever. The person with whom I have any transactions, any human dealings whatever. Not the woman only with whom I dine; not the friend only with whom I share my thoughts; not the man only whom my compassion would lift from some slough; but the woman who makes my clothes; the man who prints my book; the man who drives me in his cab; the woman who begs from me in the street. . . ; yea, even the person who condescends to me. With all and each there is a chance of doing the part of a neighbor, if in no other way yet by speaking truly, acting justly, and thinking kindly.

> We must not choose our neighbors;
>
> we must take the neighbor that God sends.

The neighbor is just the person

who is next to you at the moment,

the person with whom any business

has brought you in contact.

Thus will love spread and spread

in wider and stronger pulses

till the whole human race

will be to you sacredly lovely.

This love of our neighbor is the only door out of the dungeon of self, where we mope and mow, striking sparks, and rubbing phosphorescences out of the walls, and blowing our own breath in our own nostrils, instead of issuing to the fair sunlight of God, the sweet winds of the universe. I think my consciousness is myself; whereas my life consists in the inbreathing of God, and the consciousness of the universe of truth. To have myself, to know myself, to enjoy myself, I call life; whereas, if I would forget myself, tenfold would be my life in God and my neighbors.

The region of human life is a spiritual region. God, my friends, my neighbors, my sisters and brothers all, is the wide world in which alone my spirit can find room. Myself is my dungeon. If I feels it not now, I will yet feel it one day—feel it as a living soul would feel being prisoned in a dead body, wrapped in sevenfold cerements, and buried in a stone-ribbed vault.

My life is not in knowing that I live, but in loving all forms of life. I am made for the All, for God, who is the All, is my life. And the essential joy of my life lies abroad in the liberty of the All. My delights, like those of the Ideal Wisdom, are with other humans. My health is in the body of which the Son of Humanity is the head. The whole region of life is open to me—nay, even more, I must live in it or perish.

The part of the philanthropist is indeed a dangerous one;

and the person who would do her neighbor good

must first study how not to do him evil,

and must begin by pulling the beam out of her own eye.

It is not good at all

to do everything for those you love

and not give them a share in the doing.

It's not kind. It's making too much of yourself.

Nor thus shall we lose the consciousness of well-being.

Far deeper and more complete,

God and our neighbor will flash it back upon us—pure as life.

All true love makes abler to love.

It is only false love,

the love of those who take their own meanest selfishness,

their own pleasure in being loved, for love,

that shrinks and narrows the soul.

Love indeed is the highest in all truth.

Love is the first comforter, and where love and truth speak, the love will be felt where the truth is never perceived. . . and the pressure of a hand, a kiss, the caress of a child, will do more to save sometimes than the wisest argument, even rightly understood. Love alone is wisdom, love alone is power; and where love seems to faint it is where self has stepped between and dulled the potency of its rays.

The thing most alien to the true idea of humanity

is the notion that our well-being lies in surpassing others.

We have to rise above ourselves, not above our neighbors;

to take all the good "of" them, not "from,"

and give them all our good in return.

That which cannot be freely shared,

can never be possessed.

Nowhere but in other lives can we breathe. Only by the reflex of other lives can we ripen our specialties, develop the idea of our unique selves, the individuality that distinguishes us from every other.

Why should we love our enemies? The deepest reason for this we cannot put in words, for it lies in the absolute reality of their being, where our enemies are of one nature with us, even of the divine nature.

It is by virtue of the divine essence which is in them, that pure essential humanity, that we call our enemies men and women. It is this humanity that we are to love—a something, I say, deeper altogether than and independent of the region of hate. It is the humanity that originates the claim of neighborhood; the neighborhood only determines the occasion of its exercise.

If it is impossible, as I believe, without love to be just, much more cannot justice co-exist with hate. The pure eye for the true vision of another's claims can only go with the loving heart. . . . It is hard enough to be just to our friends; and how shall our enemies fare with us? For justice demands that we shall think rightly of our neighbor as certainly as that we shall neither steal his goods nor bear false witness against her.

Love is the law of our condition.

Without love we can no more render justice

than we can keep a straight line walking in the dark.

The eye is not single,

and the body is not full of light.

No one who is even indifferent to the other person

can recognize the claims which humanity has.

Nay, the very indifference itself is an injustice.

The question must be put to us each, "Is my neighbor indeed my enemy, or am I my neighbor's enemy, and so take her to be mine?—awful thought! Or, if she be mine, am not I hers? Am I not refusing to acknowledge the child of the kingdom within her bosom, so killing the child of the kingdom within my own?"

The Truth is at work.

In the faith of this, let us love our enemies now,

accepting God's work in them,

so that we are no longer their enemies,

in as much as they are not ours.

I have my message of my great Lord,

you have yours.

For the infinitude of God can only begin and only go on to be revealed, through God's infinitely differing creatures—all capable of wondering at, admiring, and loving each other, and so bound all in one in God, each to the others revealing Divinity. For every human being is like a facet cut in the great diamond to which I may dare liken the One who likens his kingdom to a pearl. Every man, woman, child—for the incomplete also God's, and in its very incompleteness reveals God as a progressive worker in Creation—is a revealer of God.

Each will regard the other as a prophet, and look to him for what the Lord hath spoken. Each, as a high priest returning from his Holy of Holies, will bring from her communion some glad tidings, some gospel of truth, which, when spoken, her neighbors shall receive and understand. Each will behold in the other a marvel of revelation, a present son or daughter of the Most High, come forth from God to reveal God afresh.

In God each will draw nigh to each.

I say, then, that every one of us is something that the other is not, and therefore knows some thing—it may be without knowing that he knows it—which no one else knows; and that it is every one's business, as one of the kingdom of light, and inheritor in it all, to give her portion to the rest; for we are one family, with God at the head and the heart of it, and Jesus Christ, our elder brother, teaching us of the Creator.

V

Transformation

If we will but let our God work with us,

there can be no limit to God's enlargement of our existence.

Transformation begins here,

in this life,

through our physical bodies.

Our body is the means of Revelation to us, the "camera" in which God's eternal shows are set forth. It is by the body that we come into contact with Nature, with other human beings, with all their revelations of God to us. It is through the body that we receive all the lessons of passion, of suffering, of love, of beauty, of science. It is through the body that we are both trained outwards from ourselves, and driven inwards into our deepest selves to find God.

There is this difference

between the growth of some human beings

and that of others:

in the one case it is a continuous dying,

in the other a continuous resurrection.

With every morn my life afresh must break

The crust of self, gathered about me fresh;

That thy wind-spirit may rush in and shake

The darkness out of me.

You thought you were going to be made

into a decent little cottage:

but God is building a palace.

And God intends to come and live there.

There is no limit to the flood of life

with which God will overflow our consciousness.

We have no conception of what life might be,

of how vast the consciousness

of which we could be made capable.

Lord Jesus, let the heart of a child be given to us,

that so we may arise from the grave of our dead selves

and die no more, but see face to face

the God of the Living.

Make not of thy heart a casket,

Opening seldom, quick to close;

But of bread a wide-mouthed basket,

Or a cup that overflows.

You will be dead

so long as you refuse to die.

Therefore all that is not beautiful in the beloved,

all that comes between and is not of love's kind,

must be destroyed.

No one can order her life, for it comes flowing over her from behind. But if it lay before us, and we could watch its current approaching from a long distance, what could we do with it before it had reached the now? In likewise a person thinks foolishly who imagines she could have done this and that with her own character and development if she had but known this and that in time.

The whole secret of progress is the doing of the thing we know. There is no other way of progress in the spiritual life; no other way of progress in the understanding of that life; only as we do, can we know.

As the world must be redeemed in a few people to begin with, so the soul is redeemed in a few of its thoughts, and works, and ways to begin with. It takes a long time to finish the new creation of this redemption.

You will yet know the dignity of your high calling, and the love of God that passes knowledge. God is not afraid of your presumptuous approach. It is you who are afraid to come near God. God does not watching over the divine dignity. . . . It is you who think so much about your souls and are so afraid of losing your life, that you dare not draw near to the Life of life, lest it should consume you.

Those are not the tears of repentance! Self-loathing is not sorrow. Yet it is good, for it marks a step in the way home, and in the father's arms the prodigal forgets the self he abominates.

My thoughts are like worms in a starless gloaming.

Lord, turn each worm into a butterfly.

No one can say he is himself,

until first he knows that he is,

and then what himself is.

In fact, nobody is himself,

and himself is nobody.

The full-grown person does not take her joy from herself. She feels joy in herself, but it comes to her from others, not from herself—from God first, and from somebody, anybody, everybody next. Her consciousness of herself is the reflex from those about her, not the result of her own turning in of her regard upon herself. It is not the contemplation of what God has made her, it is the being what God has made her, and the contemplation of what God is, and what God has made others, that gives her joy.

Those who are growing the right way,

the more they understand,

the more they wonder;

and the more they learn to do,

the more they want to do.

When we are who we are meant to be we trust in a strength which is not ours, and which we do not feel, do not even always desire; we believe in a power that seems far from us, which is yet at the root of our fatigue itself and our very need of rest—rest as far from death as is labor. To trust in the strength of God in our weakness; to say, "I am weak: so let me be: God is strong"; to seek from God who is our life, as the natural, simple cure of all that is amiss with us, power to do, and be, and live, even when we are weary—this is the victory that overcomes the world.

VI
Prayer

My prayers, my God, flow from what I am not;

I think thy answers make me what I am.

Never wait for fitter time or place to talk to God.

To wait till you go to church or to your closet

is to make God wait.

God will listen as you walk.

Anything big enough to occupy our minds

is big enough to hang a prayer on.

If I find my position, my consciousness, that of one from home, nay, that of one in some sort of prison; if I find that I can neither rule the world in which I live nor my own thoughts or desires; that I cannot quiet my passions, order my likings, determine my ends, will my growth, forget when I would, or recall what I forget; that I cannot love where I would, or hate where I would; that I am no ruler over myself; that I cannot supply my own needs, do not even always know which of my seeming needs are to be supplied, and which treated as impostors; if, in a word, my own being is everyway too much for me; if I can neither understand it, be satisfied with it, nor better it—may it not well give me pause—the pause that ends in prayer?

Communion with God is the one need of the soul beyond all other need; prayer is the beginning of that communion, and some need is the motive of that prayer. Our wants are for the sake of our coming into communion with God, our eternal need.

When the soul is hungry for the light, for the truth—when its hunger has waked its higher energies, thoroughly roused the will, and brought the soul into its highest condition, that of action, its only fitness for receiving the things of God, that action is prayer. Then God can give; then God can be as God would toward the human.

For the glory of God
is to give God.

Death is not an impervious wall;

through it, beyond it, go our prayers.

It is possible we may have some to help in the next world because we have prayed for them in this: will it not be a boon to them to have an old friend to their service? I but speculate and suggest. What I see and venture to say is this: If in God we live and move and have our being; if the very possibility of loving lies in this, that we exist in and by the live air of love, namely God, we must in this very fact be nearer to each other than by any bodily proximity or interchange of help; and if prayer is like a pulse that sets this atmosphere in motion, we must then by prayer come closer to each other than are the parts of our body by their complex nerve-telegraphy. Surely, in the Eternal, hearts are never parted! surely, through the Eternal, a heart that loves and seeks the good of another, must hold that other within reach! Surely the system of things would not be complete in relation to the best thing in it—love itself—if love had no help in prayer.

That God should hang in the thought-atmosphere

like a windmill, waiting till enough people

should combine and send out prayer

in sufficient force to turn God's outspread arms,

is an idea too absurd.

But how if the eternal, limitless Love, the unspeakable, self-forgetting God-devotion, which, demanding all, gives all, should say, "Child . . . here is a corner for you, my little one: push at this thing to get it out of the way"! How if God should say to us, "Pray on, my child; I am hearing you; it goes through me in help to the one for whom you pray. We are of one mind about it; I help and you help."

VII
Faith and Doubt

The more we trust,

the more reasonable we find it to trust.

The one who fears, Lord, to doubt,

in that fear doubts you.

With all sorts of doubts I am familiar, and the result of them is, has been, and will be, a widening of my heart and soul and mind to greater glories of the truth.

I cannot say I never doubt, nor until I hold the very heart of good as my very own in God, can I even wish not to doubt. For doubt is the hammer that breaks the windows clouded with human fancies, and lets in the pure light.

You doubt because you love truth.

Then the Old Man of the Earth stooped over the floor of the cave, raised a huge stone from it, and left it leaning. It disclosed a great hole that went plumb-down.

"That is the way," he said.

"But there are no stairs."

"You must throw yourself in. There is no other way."

Faith is a leap into the dark,

a total surrender.

Doubts remain.

Only the surrender matters.

The principal part of faith is patience.

That person is perfect in faith who can come to God in the utter dearth of feelings and desires, without a glow or an aspiration, with the weight of low thoughts, failures, neglects, and wandering forgetfulness, and say, "Thou art my refuge, because thou art my home."

People must believe what they can,

and those who believe more

must not be hard

upon those who believe less.

To believe in God our strength in the face of all seeming denial, to believe in God out of the heart of weakness and unbelief, in spite of numbness and weariness and lethargy; to believe in the wide-awake real, through all the stupefying, enervating, distorting dream; to will to wake, when the very being seems athirst for a godless repose—these are the broken steps up to the high fields where repose is but a form of strength, strength but a form of joy, joy but a form of love. "I am weak," says the true soul, "but not so weak that I would not be strong; not so sleepy that I would not see the sun rise; not so lame but that I would walk! Thanks be to the One who perfects strength in weakness, and gives to us who are beloved while we sleep!"

"Could you not give me some sign, or tell me something about you that never changes, or some other way to know you, or thing to know you by?"

"No, Curdie: that would be to keep you from knowing me. You must know me in quite another way from that. It would not be the least use to you or me either if I were to make you know me in that way. It would be but to know the sign of me—not to know me myself."

What you love you already believe enough to put it to the proof of trial. My life is such a proving; and the proof is so promising that it fills me with the happiest hope. To prove with your brains the thing you love, would be to deck the garments of salvation with a useless fringe. Shall I search heaven and earth for proof that my wife is a good and lovely woman? The signs of it are everywhere; the proofs of it nowhere.

Faith is that which, knowing the Lord's will, goes and does it; or, not knowing it, stands and waits, content in ignorance as in knowledge, because God wills; neither pressing into the hidden future, nor careless of the knowledge which opens the path of action. It is its noblest exercise to act with uncertainty of the result, when the duty itself is certain, or even when a course seems with strong probability to be duty.

Fold the arms of thy faith, and wait in quietness until light goes up in thy darkness. Fold the arms of thy Faith I say, but not of thy Action: think of something that you ought to do, and go and do it, if it be but the sweeping of a room, or the preparing of a meal, or a visit to a friend.

Heed not your feelings:

Do your work.

Faith give dimension to life's vista;

more, it is the depth of another dimension.

The universe would be to me no more than a pasteboard scene, all surface and no deepness, on the stage, if I did not hope in God. I will not say *believe*, for that is a big word, and it means so much more than my low beginnings of confidence. But a little faith may wake a great big hope, and I look for great things from the One whose perfection breathed me out that I might be a perfect thing one day.

"The care that is filling your mind at this moment, or but waiting till you lay the book aside to leap upon you—that need which is no need, is a demon sucking at the spring of your life."

"No; mine is a reasonable care—an unavoidable care, indeed!"

"Is it something you have to do this very moment?"

"No."

"Then you are allowing it to usurp the place of something that is required of you this moment!"

"There is nothing required of me at this moment."

"Nay, but there is—the greatest thing that can be required of a person."

"And what is that?"

"Trust in the living God. The divine will is your life."

Tomorrow makes today's whole head sick,

its whole heart faint.

When we should be still,

or sleeping, or dreaming,

we are fretting about an hour

that lies a half sun's journey away!

VIII
Work and Action

It is but from the very step upon which one stands

that one can move to the next.

Do the things you know,

and you shall learn the truth you need to know.

The only way to learn the rules of anything practical is to begin to do the thing. We have enough knowledge in us . . . to begin anything requested of us. The sole way to deal with the profoundest mystery . . . is to begin to do some duty revealed by it.

The person who cannot invent

will never discover.

God left the world unfinished

for humans to work their skill upon.

God left the electricity still in the cloud,

the oil still in the earth.

It is a fine thing to work—

the finest thing in the world,

if it comes of love, as God's work does.

I believe the day will come when the word "duty" will be forgotten, except as a matter of history, when the heart, the whole being, will be so filled with love to the right thing, not because it is a duty laid upon us to do, but just because it is what it is—the loveliness of God—that we shall never think of its being our duty, but to make haste with our whole nature to do it with gladness and song.

We are like God with whom there is no past or future, with whom a day is as a thousand years, and a thousand years as one day, when we do our work in the great present, leaving both past and future to the One to whom they are ever present, and fearing nothing, because God is in our future as much as God is in our past, as much as, and far more than we can feel God to be in our present. Partakers thus of the divine nature, resting in that perfect All-in-all in whom our nature is eternal too, we walk without fear, full of hope and courage and strength to do the divine will, waiting for the endless good which God is always giving as fast as the divine creativity can get us able to take it.

Doubt may be a poor encouragement to do anything,

but it is a bad reason for doing nothing.

Our labors must pass like the sunrises and sunsets of the world.
The next thing, not the last must be our care.

Labor is grand officer in the palace of Art; that at the root of all ease lies slow, and, for long, profitless-seeming labor, as at the root of all grace lies strength; that ease is the lovely result of forgotten toil, sunk into the spirit, and making it strong and ready; that never worthy improvisation flowed from brain of poet or musician unused to perfect his work with honest labor; that the very disappearance of toil is by the immolating hand of toil itself. The person only who bears her own burden can bear the burden of another; he only who has labored shall dwell at ease, or help others from the mire to the rock.

What God may hereafter require of you, you must not give yourself the least trouble about. Everything God gives you to do, you must do as well as ever you can, and that is the best possible preparation for what God may want you to do next.

If people would but do what they have to do,

they would always find themselves ready

for what came next.

Work is not always required.

There is such a thing

as sacred idleness.

IX
Troubles

The lighting and thunder, they go and they come:

But the stars and the stillness are always at home.

Of all things let us avoid the false refuge of a weary collapse, a hopeless yielding to things as they are. It is the life in us that is discontented; we need more of what is discontented, not more of the cause of its discontent. Discontent, I repeat, is the life in us that has not enough of itself, is not enough to itself, so calls for more. He has the victory who, in the midst of pain and weakness, cries out, not for death, not for the repose of forgetfulness, but for strength to fight; for more power, more consciousness of being, more God in him.

To fight despair is the truth,

and the only way.

Come, then, affliction, if God wills,

and be my frowning friend.

A friend that frowns is better than a smiling enemy.

He came to himself in the arms of a strange woman, who had taken him up, and was carrying him home. The name of the woman was Sorrow—a wondering woman, a kind of gypsy, always going about the world, and picking up lost things. Nobody likes her, hardly anybody is civil to her; but when she has set anybody down and is gone, there is often a look of affection and wonder and gratitude sent after her. For all that, however, very few are glad to be found by her again.

When I can no more stir my soul to move,

and life is but the ashes of a fire;

when I can but remember

that my heart once used to live and love,

long and aspire—O, be thou then the first,

the one thou art; be thou the calling,

before all answering love,

and in me wake hope, fear, boundless desire.

It was foolish indeed—

thus to run farther and farther

from all who could help her,

as if she had been seeking a fit spot

for the goblin creature to eat her in at his leisure;

but that is the way fear serves us:

it always sides with the thing we are afraid of.

Yet I know that good is coming to me—that good is always coming; though few have at all times the simplicity and the courage to believe it. What we call evil, is the only and best shape, which, for the person and his condition at the time, could be assumed by the best good.

To be left alone

is not always to be forsaken.

God begs you to leave the future to God

and mind the present.

It has been well said that nobody ever sank under the burden of the day. It is when tomorrow's burden is added to the burden of today that the weight is more than anyone can bear. Never load yourselves so, my friends. If you find yourselves so loaded, at least remember this is your own doing, not God's.

Low-sunk life imagines itself weary of life, but it is death, not life, it is weary of. Let us in all the troubles of life remember—that our one lack is life—that what we need is more life—more of the life-making presence in us making us more, and more largely, alive. When most oppressed, when most weary of life, as our unbelief would phrase it, let us bethink ourselves that it is in truth the inroad and presence of death we are weary of. When most inclined to sleep, let us rouse ourselves to live. Of all things let us avoid the false refuge of a weary collapse, a hopeless yielding to things as they are. It is the life in us that is discontented; we need more of what is discontented, not more of the cause of its discontent.

Discontent, I repeat, is the life in us that has not enough of itself, is not enough to itself, so calls for more. That person has the victory who, in the midst of pain and weakness, cries out, not for death, not for the repose of forgetfulness, but for strength to fight; for more power, more consciousness of being, more God.

I found cheerfulness itself to be like life itself—not to be created by any argument. Afterwards I learned, that the best way to manage some kinds of painful thoughts, is to dare them to do their worst; to let them lie and gnaw at your heart till they are tired; and you find you still have a residue of life they cannot kill.

Every tempest

is but an assault in the siege of Love.

The terror of God

is but the other side of His love;

it is love outside, that would be inside.

Christianity vs.
the Mind of Christ

Division has done more to hide Christ

than all the infidelity that has ever been spoken.

Till we begin to learn . . . that the only way to serve God in any real sense of the word is to serve our neighbor, we may have knocked at the wicket-gate, but I doubt if we have got one foot across the threshold of the Kingdom.

Truth is truth, whether from the lips of Jesus or Balaam. But, in its deepest sense, the truth is a condition of heart, soul, mind, and strength towards God and toward others—not an utterance, not even a right form of words.

I firmly believe people have hitherto
been a great deal too much taken up about doctrine
and far too little about practice.

The word doctrine, as used in the Bible, means teaching of duty, not theory. We are far too anxious to be definite and to have finished, well-polished, sharp-edged systems—forgetting that the more perfect a theory about the infinite, the surer it is to be wrong, the more impossible it is to be right.

Jesus Christ: the everyday life of the world,

whose presence is just as needful in ordinary life,

as at what so many of the clergy call the altar.

When the Lord is known as the heart of every joy,

as well as the refuge from every sorrow,

then the altar will be known for what it is—

an ecclesiastical antique.

I would never speak about faith, but speak about the Lord himself—not theologically, as to the why and wherefore of his death—but as he showed himself in his life on earth, full of grace, love, beauty, tenderness and truth. Then the needy heart cannot help hoping and trusting in him, and having faith, without ever thinking about faith. How a human heart with human feelings and necessities is ever to put confidence in the theological phantom which is commonly called Christ in our pulpits, I do not know. It is commonly a miserable representation of him who spent thirty-three years on our Earth, living himself into the hearts and souls of men, and thus manifesting God to them.

How have we learned Christ?

It ought to be a startling thought,

that we may have learned him wrong:

his place is occupied by a false Christ, hard to exorcise!

The point is, whether we have learned Christ as he taught himself, or as people have taught him who thought they understood, but did not understand him. Do we think we know him—with notions fleshly, after low, mean human fancies and explanations, or do we indeed know him—after the spirit, in our measure as God knows him? Have we learned Christ in false statements and corrupted lessons about him, or have we learned *himself*? Nay, true or false, is only our brain full of things concerning him, or does he dwell himself in our hearts, a learned, and ever-being-learned lesson, the power of our life?

Some of you say we must trust in the finished work of Christ; or again, our faith must be in the merits of Christ—in the atonement he has made—in the blood he has shed: all these statements are a simple repudiation of the living Lord, *in whom* we are told to believe, who, by his presence with and in us, and our obedience to him, lifts us out of darkness into light, leads us from the kingdom of Satan into the glorious liberty of the children of God. With such teaching I have had a lifelong acquaintance, and declare it most miserably false.

No manner or amount of belief ABOUT Christ

is the faith of the New Testament.

Growth was a doctrine unembodied in his creed; he turned from everything new, no matter how harmonious with the old, in freezing disapprobation; he recognized no element in God or nature which could not be reasoned about after the forms of conservative philosophy. In religion he regarded everything not only as settled, but as understood; but seemed aware of no call in relation to truth but to bark at any one who showed the least anxiety to discover it. What truth he held himself, he held as a sack holds corn—not even as a worm holds earth.

Even if your plan, your theories, were absolutely true, the holding of them with sincerity, the trusting in this or that about Christ, or in anything he did or could do, the trusting in anything but himself, his own living self, is a delusion. Many will grant this heartily, and yet the moment you come to talk with them, you find they insist that to believe in Christ is to believe in the atonement, meaning by that only and altogether their special theory about the atonement; and when you say we must believe in the atoning Christ, and cannot possibly believe in any theory concerning the atonement, they go away and denounce you, saying, "He does not believe in the atonement!" If I explain the atonement otherwise than they explain it, they assert that I deny the atonement; nor count it of any consequence that I say I believe in the atoner with my whole heart, and soul, and strength, and mind.

I have no desire to change the opinion of man or woman. Let everyone for me hold what he pleases. But I would do my utmost to disable such as think correct opinion essential to salvation from laying any other burden on the shoulders of true men and women than the yoke of their master; and such burden, if already oppressing any, I would gladly lift. Let the Lord himself teach them, I say. A person who has not the mind of Christ—and no one has the mind of Christ except person who makes it her business to obey him—cannot have correct opinions concerning him.

One chief cause of unbelief in the world is,

that those who have seen something of the glory of Christ,

set themselves to theorize concerning him

rather than to obey him.

They have not taught Christ, but *about* Christ. More eager after credible theory than after doing the truth, they have speculated in a condition of heart in which it was impossible they should understand; they have presumed to explain a Christ whom years and years of obedience could alone have made them able to comprehend. Such, naturally, press their theories, insisting on their thinking about Christ as they think, instead of urging them to go to Christ to be taught by him whatever he chooses to teach them.

"This then is the message," John says, "which we have heard of him, and declare unto you, that God is light, and in him is no darkness at all." Ah, my heart, this is indeed the good news! This is a gospel! If God be light, what more, what else can I seek than God, than Godself! Away with your doctrines! Away with your salvation from the "justice" of a God whom it is a horror to imagine! Away with your iron cages of false metaphysics! I am saved—for God is light!

How terribly, then, have the theologians misrepresented God! Nearly all of them represent him as a great King on a grand throne, thinking how grand he is, and making it the business of his being and the end of his universe to keep up his glory, wielding the bolts of a Jupiter against them that take his name in vain. They would not allow this, but follow out what they say, and it comes much to this. Brothers, have you found our king? There he is, kissing little children and saying they are like God. There he is at table with the head of a fisherman lying on his bosom, and somewhat heavy at heart that even he, the beloved disciple, cannot yet understand him well. The simplest peasant who loves his children and his sheep were—no, not a truer, for the other is false, but—a true type of our God beside that monstrosity of a monarch.

A stick, or a stone, or a devil, is all that some of our fellow humans have to believe in: the person who believes in a God not altogether unselfish and good, a God who does not do all possible for Creation, belongs to the same class; this is not the God who made the heaven and the earth and the sea and the fountains of water—not the God revealed in Christ. If a person see in God any darkness at all, and especially if he defend that darkness, attempting to justify it as one who respects the person of God, I cannot but think . . . if he had been strenuously obeying Jesus, he would ere now have received the truth that God is light, and in God is no darkness—a truth which is not acknowledged by calling the darkness attributed to God light, and the candle of the Lord in the soul of humanity darkness. It is one thing to believe that God can do nothing wrong, quite another to call right whatever presumption one may attribute to God.

To let their light shine, not to force on them their interpretations of God's designs, is the duty of Christians toward their fellow humans. If you who set yourselves to explain the theory of Christianity, had set yourselves instead to do the will of the Master, the one object for which the Gospel was preached to you, how different would now be the condition of that portion of the world with which you come into contact!

You would have been thinking far less

of serving God on Sunday,

and far more of serving your neighbor in the week.

To love righteousness is to make it grow,

not to avenge it.

The one only thing truly to reconcile all differences is, to walk in the light. So St. Paul teaches us in his epistle to the Philippians, the third chapter and sixteenth verse. . . . In such walking, and in such walking only, love will grow, truth will grow; the soul, then first in its genuine element and true relation towards God, will see into reality that was before but a blank to it; and the One who has promised to teach, will teach abundantly. Faster and faster will the glory of the Lord dawn upon the hearts and minds of people so walking

What boy, however fain to be a disciple of Christ and a child of God, would prefer a sermon to his glorious kite, that divinest of toys, with God for his playmate, in the blue wind that tossed it hither and thither in the golden void! He might be ready to part with kite and wind and sun, and go down to the grave for his brothers—but surely not that they might be admitted to an everlasting prayer-meeting!

For my own part, I rejoice to think that there will be neither church nor chapel in the high countries; yea, that there will be nothing there called religion, and no law but the perfect law of liberty. For how should there be law or religion where every throb of the heart says God! where every song-throat is eager with thanksgiving! where such a tumult of glad waters is for ever bursting from beneath the throne of God, the tears of the gladness of the universe!

Religion?

Where will be the room for it,

when the essence of every thought must be God?

There is another kind of forsaking that may fall to the lot of some, and which they may find very difficult: the forsaking of such notions of God and Christ as they were taught in their youth—which they held, nor could help holding, at such time as they began to believe—which they have begun to doubt the truth, but to cast which away seems like parting with every assurance of safety.

There are so-called doctrines long accepted of good people, which how any who love God can hold, except indeed by fast closing of the spiritual eyes, I find it hard to understand.

Good souls many will one day be horrified at the things they now believe of God.

We will come to see that we must follow NO doctrine,

be it true as human word could state it,

but the living Truth, Christ the person.

XI

The Unconscious

The Greatest Forces

lie in the region of the uncomprehended.

If a dream reveal a principle,

that principle is a revelation

and the dream

is neither more nor less valuable

than a waking thought that does the same.

"Go down that stair, and it will bring you to him," said the old man of the sea.

With humble thanks Tangle took her leave. She went down the winding stair, till she began to fear there was no end to it. Still down and down it went, rough and broken, with springs of water bursting out of the rocks and running down the steps beside her. It was quite dark about her, and yet she could see. For after being in that bath, people's eyes always give out a light they can see by. There were no creeping things in the way. All was safe and pleasant, though so dark and damp and deep.

Strange dim memories, which will not abide identification, often, through misty windows of the past, look out upon me in the broad daylight. . . . It may be, notwithstanding, that, when most awake, I am only dreaming the more! But when I wake at last into that life which, as a mother her child, carries this life in its bosom, I shall know that I wake, and shall doubt no more.

I wait; asleep or awake, I wait.

Thank God

for the night and darkness and sleep

in which good things draw nigh

like God's thieves,

and steal themselves in—water into wells,

and peace and hope and courage

into human minds.

In knowing God is life and its gladness.

The secret of your own heart you can never know;

but you can know the One who knows its secret.

It is only in God

that the soul has room.

XII

Animals and Nature

There is nothing in the whole universe

that we can call lovely,

that moves our heart or soul,

but it is a little shimmer of the heart of Christ.

God's creative hand is still at work

in forest and field,

in all the natural world.

My interest in its loveliness would vanish, I should feel that the soul was out of it, if you could persuade me that God had ceased to care for the daisy, and now cared for something else instead. The faces of some flowers lead me back to the heart of God; and, as a child of Divinity, I hope I feel, in my lowly degree, what God felt and said, when brooding over them, "They are good"; that is, "They are what I mean."

None of the creatures came from God's *hands*. Perhaps the precious things of the earth, the coal and the diamonds, the iron and clay and gold, may be said to have come from the divine hands; but the live things come from God's heart— from near the same region whence ourselves we came.

Your dog, your horse tells you about the One
who cares for all creatures.

How much my horse may, in his own fashion—that is, God's equine way—know of God, I cannot tell, because he cannot tell. Also, we do not know what the horses know, because they are horses, and we are at best, in relation to them, only horsemen. But the ways of God go into the depths yet unrevealed to us; God knows the horses and dogs as we cannot know them, because we are not yet pure children of God.

When through our redemption, as Paul teaches, the redemption of these lower brothers and sisters shall have come, then we shall understand each other better. But now the Lord of Life has to look on at the willful torture of multitudes of God creatures. It must be that offences come, but woe unto that person by whom they come! The Lord may seem not to heed, but God sees and knows.

The ways of God go down into microscopic depths,

as well as up into telescopic heights—

and with more marvel,

for there lie the beginnings of life.

It is live things that God cares most about—

not things set down in a book, or in memory,

or embalmed in the joy of knowledge,

but things lifting up the heart,

things active in an active will.

A mountain is a strange and awful thing. In old times, without knowing so much of their strangeness and awfulness as we do, people were yet more afraid of mountains. But then somehow they had not come to see how beautiful they are as well as awful, and they hated them—and what people hate they must fear. Now that we have learned to look at them with admiration, perhaps we do not feel quite awe enough of them. To me they are beautiful terrors.

Sky and wind and water and birds and trees said to him, "Forget thyself, and we will think of thee. Sing no more to thyself thy foolish songs of decay, and we will all sing to thee of love and hope and faith and resurrection." Earth and air had grown full of hints and sparkles and vital motions, as if between them and his soul an abiding community of fundamental existence had manifested itself.

The sky soothed him then, he knew not how. Nature bears expressions that can influence, though unconsciously to them, the most ignorant and hopeless of God's children.

For the face of nature

is the face of God.

XIII

Old Age, Death, and the World to Come

All that is not God is death.

Age is not all decay;

it is the ripening, the swelling,

of the fresh life within,

that withers and bursts the husk.

It is so silly of people to fancy that old age means crooked-ness and witheredness and feebleness and sticks and spec-tacles and rheumatism and forgetfulness! . . . The right old age means strength and beauty and mirth and courage and clear eyes.

When we are out of sympathy with the young,

then I think our work in this world is over.

The boy should enclose and keep, as his life, the old child at the heart of him, and never let it go. He must still, to be a right man, be his mother's darling, and more, his father's pride, and more.

The child is not meant to die,

but to be forever fresh born.

Happy the person

who shall be able to believe that old age itself,

with its pitiable decays and sad dreams of youth,

is … a sure sign

of the Lord's love.

THE COMING

On the earth when deep snows lie

Still the sun is in the sky,

And when most we miss his fire

He is ever drawing nigher.

In the darkest winter day,

Thou, God, art not far away;

When the nights grow colder, drearer,

Father, thou art coming nearer!

I think of death as the first pulse of the new strength, shaking itself free from the old moldy remnants of earth-garments, that it may begin in freedom the new life that grows out of the old. The caterpillar dies into the butterfly.

Every night that folds us up in darkness is a death; and those of you that have been out early, and have seen the first of the dawn, will know it—the day rises out of the night like a being that has burst its tomb and escaped into life.

The world

is full of resurrections.

How strange this fear of death is!
We are never frightened at a sunset.

"In the midst of life we are in death," said one; it is more true that in the midst of death we are in life. Life is the only reality; what people call death is but a shadow—a word for that which cannot be—a negation, owing the very idea of itself to that which it would deny. But for life there could be no death. If God were not, there would not even be nothing. Not even nothingness preceded life. Nothingness owes its very idea to existence.

We who ARE, have nothing to do with death;

our relations are alone with life.

We are vessels of life, not yet full of the wine of life; where the wine does not reach, there the clay cracks, and aches, and is distressed. Who would therefore pour out the wine that is there, instead of filling to the brim with more wine! All the being must partake of essential being; life must be assisted, upheld, comforted, every part, with life. Life is the law, the food, the necessity of life. Life is everything. Many doubtless mistake the joy of life for life itself; and, longing after the joy, languish with a thirst at once poor and inextinguishable; but even that thirst points to the one spring. These love self, not life, and self is but the shadow of life. When it is taken for life itself, and set as our center, it becomes a live death within us, a devil we worship as our god!

Let us first ask what is the use of this body of ours. It is the means of Revelation to us, the *camera* in which God's eternal shows are set forth. It is by the body that we come into contact with Nature, with our fellow humans, with all their revelations of God to us. It is through the body that we receive all the lessons of passion, of suffering, of love, of beauty, of science. It is through the body that we are both trained outwards from ourselves, and driven inwards into our deepest selves to find God. There is glory and might in this vital evanescence, this slow glacier-like flow of clothing and revealing matter, this ever uptossed rainbow of tangible humanity. It is no less of God's making than the spirit that is clothed therein.

Ah, my friends! what will resurrection or life be to me, how shall I continue to love God as I have learned to love God through you, if I find the Divine One cares so little for this human heart of mine, as to take from me the gracious visitings of your faces and forms? True, I might have a gaze at Jesus, now and then; but he would not be so good as I had thought him. And how should I see him if I could not see you? God will not take you, has not taken you from me to bury you out of my sight in the abyss of his own unfathomable being, where I cannot follow and find you, myself lost in the same awful gulf. No, our God is an unveiling, a revealing God. God will raise you from the dead, that I may behold you; that that which vanished from the earth may again stand forth, looking out of the same eyes of eternal love and truth, holding out the same mighty hand of brotherhood, the same delicate and gentle, yet strong hand of sisterhood, to me, this me that knew you and loved you in the days gone by.

I shall not care that the matter of the forms I loved a thousand years ago has returned to mingle with the sacred goings on of God's science, upon that far-off world wheeling its nursery of growing loves and wisdoms through space; I shall not care that the muscle which now sends the ichor through your veins is not formed of the very particles which once sent the blood to the pondering brain, the flashing eye, or the nervous right arm; I shall not care, I say, so long as it is yourselves that are before me, beloved; so long as through these forms I know that I look on my own, on my loving souls of the ancient time; so long as my spirits have got garments of revealing after their own old lovely fashion, garments to reveal themselves to me. The new shall then be dear as the old, and for the same reason, that it reveals the old love. And in the changes which, thank God, must take place when the mortal puts on immortality, shall we not feel that the nobler our friends are, the more they are themselves; that the more the idea of each is carried out in the perfection of beauty, the more like they are to what we thought them in our most exalted moods, to that which we saw in them in the rarest moments of profoundest communion, to that which we beheld through the veil of all their imperfections when we loved them the truest?

The beloved pass from our sight, but they pass not from thine, God. This that we call death, is but a form in the eyes of humans. It looks something final, an awful cessation, an utter change. It seems not probable that there is anything beyond. But if God could see us before we were, and make us after the divine ideal, that we shall have passed from the eyes of our friends can be no argument that God beholds us no longer. Let the change be ever so great, ever so imposing; let the unseen life be ever so vague to our conception, it is not against reason to hope that God could see Abraham, after Isaac had ceased to see him; saw Isaac after Jacob ceased to see him; saw Jacob after some of the Sadducees had begun to doubt whether there ever had been a Jacob at all. God remembers them; that is, God carries them in the divine mind: the person of whom God thinks, lives.

All live unto God.

We may say, then,

that whatever is the source of joy or love,

whatever is pure and strong,

whatever wakes aspiration,

whatever lifts us out of selfishness,

whatever is beautiful or admirable—

in a word, whatever is of the light—

must make a part, however small

it may then prove to be in its proportion,

of the inheritance of the saints in the light.

"You have tasted death now," said the Old Man.

"Is it good?"

"It is good," said Mossy.

"It is better than life."

"No," said the Old Man,

"it is only more life."

Whatever the place be like, one thing is certain, that there will be endless, infinite atonement, ever-growing love. Certain too it is that whatever the divinely human heart desires, it shall not desire in vain. The light which is God, and which is our inheritance because we are the children of God, insures these things.

For the heart which desires

is made thus to desire.

XIV

Heart's Desires
and the Will of God

We are dwellers in a divine universe

where no desires are in vain—

if only they be large and true enough.

There are good things God must delay giving

until the child has a pocket to hold them—

till God gets the child to make that pocket.

God must first make her fit to receive and to have.

There is no part of our nature

that shall not be satisfied—and that not by lessening it,

but by enlarging it to embrace

an ever-enlarging enough.

For the divine will is the root of all God's children's gladness, of all their laughter and merriment. The child that loves the will of the God, is at the heart of things; his will is "with" the motion of the eternal wheels; the eyes of all those wheels are opened upon him, and he knows whence he came. Happy and fearless and hopeful, he knows himself the child of the One from whom he came, and his peace and joy break out in light. He rises and shines.

Bliss creative and energetic there is none other,

on earth or in heaven, than the will of God.

It is one and the same.

Have patience, my love. Your heart's deepest desire must be the divine will, for God cannot have made you so that your heart should run counter to that will; let God have way with you, and God will give you your desire. To that end goes the divine path. God delights in us; so soon as we can be indulged without ruin, God will heap upon us our desires; they are God's desires too.

What a person likes best may be God's will,

may be the voice of the Spirit striving with the human spirit,

not against it.

God is the origin of both need and supply . . . the abundant giver of the good things. Right gloriously he meets our needs! The story of Jesus is the heart of God's answer, not primarily to the prayers, but to the divine necessities of the children God has sent out into the universe.

The soul God made is thus hungering,

though the selfish, usurping self,

which is its consciousness,

is hungering only after low and selfish things,

ever trying, but in vain,

to fill its mean, narrow content,

with husks too poor

for its poverty-stricken desires.

IV

The Heart's Home

When we have God,

all is holy, and we are at home.

Christ is both our home—
and the way home.

Christ is the way out, and the way in; the way from slavery, conscious or unconscious, into liberty; the way from the unhomeliness of things to the home we desire but do not know; the way from the stormy skirts of the Father's garments to the peace of the divine bosom. To picture Christ, we need not only endless figures, but sometimes quite opposing figures: he is not only the door of the sheepfold, but the shepherd of the sheep; he is not only the way, but the leader in the way, the rock that followed, and the captain of our salvation. We must become as little children, and Christ must be born in us; we must learn of him, and the one lesson he has to give is himself.

The one bliss of the universe

is the presence of God—

which is simply God being to the human,

and felt by the human as being,

that which in our own nature God is—

the indwelling power of divine life.

I think we shall come at length to feel all places,

as all times and all spaces, venerable,

because they are the outcome

of the eternal nature

and the eternal thought.

We thank you for yourself.

Be what you are —

our root and life,

our beginning and end, our all in all.

Come home to us.

You live; therefore we live.

In your light we see.

You ARE—

that is all our song.

CHECK OUT THIS OTHER TITLE FROM
ΛΝΛϽϽϽλΛΚΛ BOOKS

Hazelnuts of Grace:
Selections from Julian of Norwich
Price: $12.95 Paperback
5 x 7 inches
152 pages
ISBN: 978-1-937211-10-3

The Spirit showed me a tiny thing the size of a hazelnut,
as round as a ball and so small I could hold it in the palm of my hand.
I . . . wondered, "What is this?" The answer came to me:
"This is everything that has been made. This is all Creation."
It was so small that I marveled it could endure;
such a tiny thing seemed likely to simply fall into nothingness.
Again the answer came to my thoughts:
"It lasts, and it will always last, because God loves it."

These selections taken from *All Shall Be Well*, Anamchara
Books' modern-language version of the complete revelation
of Julian of Norwich, are arranged thematically, bite-size
thoughts to be read slowly, one at a time. This is the sort of
book that's meant to be picked up for five minutes and put
down again . . . while a kernel of truth lingers in your mind,
transforming your thoughts. Each short selection contains
within it Julian's amazing message:

all shall be well
because God's love sustains our world.

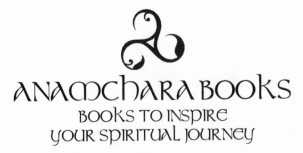

ANAMCHARA BOOKS
BOOKS TO INSPIRE
YOUR SPIRITUAL JOURNEY

In Celtic Christianity, an *anamchara* is a soul friend, a companion and mentor (often across the miles and the years) on the spiritual journey. Soul friendship entails a commitment to both accept and challenge, to reach across all divisions in a search for the wisdom and truth at the heart of our lives.

At Anamchara Books, we are committed to creating a community of soul friends by publishing books that lead us into deeper relationships with God, the Earth, and each other. These books connect us with the great mystics of the past, as well as with more modern spiritual thinkers. They are designed to build bridges, shaping an inclusive spirituality where we all can grow.

You can order our books at **www.AnamcharaBooks.com**. Check out our site to read opinions and perspectives from our editorial staff on our Soul Friends blog. You can also submit your own blog posts by emailing **info@AnamcharaBooks.com** with "Blog Entry for Soul Friends" in the subject line. To find out more about Anamchara Books and connect with others on their own spiritual journeys, visit **www.AnamcharaBooks.com** today.

ANAMCHARA BOOKS
220 Front Street
Vestal, New York 13850
(607) 785-1578
www.AnamcharaBooks.com

8516071R0